CURTAIN PRINCIPLE
(A BROADER VIEW)

BY

ARYAN SANGEETH

For Google Form help, Scan the above QR Code

ARYAN BOOKS INDIA

<u>First Edition</u>

January 2023

<u>NOTICE</u>

- The book is available as eBook, paperback and hardcover.
- Price may vary according to the location where it is sold.
- The book is currently available only in English language.
- The author wrote this book in India.
- The author is not responsible for any damage or torn pages of the book.
- The book is based on author's assumptions and observations.
- The author has not provided any destructive criticism.
- The book does not use any images or photos from third party sites.
- The book should not be edited or republished without the prior permission of the author/publisher.
- There are no advertisements in the book.

PREFACE

You may know that each object and person is assigned a 'rank' that determines the position of that object/person in the society. The 'rank' is given due to many reasons. The social identity like majority's religion, caste, class, race, age, gender and language may play an important role in determining the rank of a human while content, promotion, use, rating and review determines the rank of an object. The common criteria that determine the rank of a human as well as of object are merit and luck. But the ranking is not permanent and it is subjected to change. The object/person with a lower rank may overcome the object/person with a higher rank to get the higher rank for itself. This is called 'Curtain Principle'.

Thus, this book 'Curtain Principle' explains how this principle governs all the aspects of the society ranging from a living to a non-living thing. It also shows how this principle is very much linked to 'Survival of the fittest' (not to be confused with Herbert

Spencer's concept in biology) and theory of international relations. In other words, you will see that 'IR approaches' and 'Survival of the fittest' are the sub-branches of 'Curtain Principle' after you read the entire book. In fact, the whole world depends on the 'Curtain Principle' to explain the relationship among people and objects that lead to a 'ranking' system. At the end of the book, you will get to know the solutions to the Curtain Principle or what can be done to bring more equality and reduce the influence of the 'Curtain Principle'.

-Author

ACKNOWLEDGEMENTS

I thank my father, Dr. Sangeeth D Rajan for giving me consent to publish this book. My sincere thanks also extend to my mother, Dr. Anju Sangeeth for supervising and coordinating the work. I acknowledge the efforts of my brother, Arjun Sangeeth in taking a critical view of my book and helping me to find answers to many questions. I also thank the readers of my book for their constant support to my work.

CONTENTS

Dedicated To,

My family, relatives (like cousins) and close friends...

CHAPTER- 1

MICRO UNITS OF CURTAINING

Here, the word 'Curtain' does not mean 'a screen of heavy cloth that is raised at the front of stage'. It is also not a 'curtain' used in the window of a house. Instead, the word 'curtain' here means the shutdown of one object/person and opening of the other. The Curtain Principle states that in a competitive world, any person, organization or thing regardless of its character tries to curtain the other for gaining self-significance. Everything does not survive for long time. It may be challenged by another object. So, over a period of time, the initial object of importance may be forgotten or side-lined due to the arrival of new object on the scene. Let us understand this in detail by exploring the micro-units of curtaining. They are as follows:

1. Family

The smallest unit where 'Curtain Principle' takes place is your family. In family, the 'Curtain Principle' is generally agreed upon through a consensus. This can happen in two ways:

> (a) If it is a joint family, the eldest member may be the head of the household. After his/her death, the next eldest person after him/her assumes the rank of head of the household.
>
> (b) If it is a nuclear family that follows matriarchal system, then a person's mother would be the head of the household. If the mother dies before the others in the family, then father takes the role of a mother to become the head of household.

This type of curtaining is not harmful as this ensures smooth functioning of a family. There are some other cases of curtaining too such as:

> (a) A child may be asked by his/her parents to get educated more than the parents or get a job at the rank higher than his/her own parents.

(b) If the child's parents have done an inter-caste marriage, the child can opt a caste which gives him/her a higher rank in the society. If the mother is from upper caste and father is from lower caste, the child may opt mother's caste and curtain his/her father. But this curtaining has declined nowadays as a child is keen on taking the caste that provides him/her the reservation of seats in jobs and educational institutions.

2. <u>Team</u>

(a) If you are the captain of any game which you play at a particular point of time, you may be well knowing that you will not continue to be the captain till your death. The equality of opportunity opens the gate for the curtain principle. It is also facilitated by the generational identities and the spirit of the youth.

(b) This also applies to a higher post such as CEO in an organization which is appointed only for a specific tenure.

Impacts:

(a) Most of the CEOs will not prefer to return to an ordinary employee of a company. They will instead choose to resign and join some other company as CEO. If the freedom of the person is restricted from joining other company after a post of CEO, then he will choose to retire forever. This is done to protect one's dignity from insult by curtain principle.

(b) The Curtain Principle however leaves a residue in the form of a title such as 'former', 'first/any number' or 'respected'.

(c) It is also observed that the curtain principle cannot erase the works done by the person who has been curtained. The history is recorded and thus, it remains as an impression on future.

3. <u>Individual</u>

The mind of a person is also curtained with changing circumstances. The priorities also change with time thus altering the rank of thoughts. There are two kinds of Curtain Principle for an individual. They are:

(a) 'Opportunity cost'

For example, one has to choose between mango and apple. Assume that the cost of 1 small mango is of 2 big apples. The initial decision would be to buy a mango as it is summer season and he wanted the taste of it. But when the person reaches the market, he may change his decision within seconds because he may feel very hungry at that time forcing him to buy 2 big apples instead of a small mango. Here, the priority shifted from taste to hunger.

(b) Ethics

For instance, you have an exam and your mother ask to visit her the same day. When your mother requests a visit when she is in healthy condition, you would normally choose exam over your mother and then go some other day. But when your mother is about to die in the bed and calls to see you for last time in her life, you would leave your exam for your mother if you are a loving son.

4. <u>Community</u>

The community can be religious or linguistic. In case of religion, take the example of Hinduism. It was called Vedic religion in ancient India which focused on various types of sacrifice. It became bhakti religion in medieval India which led to the division within Hinduism into Vaishnavism, Shaivism and Shaktism. In modern India, smartism increased in Hinduism and different tribal religions also came to be associated with Hinduism. This change is brought by reformers to challenge the existing traditions through curtain principle.

In linguistic community, the curtain principle brings changes in style of speaking and in the script as observed in Malayalam, a scheduled language of the Indian Constitution. Curtain Principle leads the evolution of new dialects which is clearly proven in Hindi language.

TECHNOLOGY CHANGES BY CURTAIN PRINCIPLE

In this section, we do not discuss about all the technological changes throughout the centuries which you can find in any book. Instead, we will emphasize the role of Curtain Principle in bringing these changes.

1. The Curtain Principle increases the speed of changes in technology. In this competitive world, rapid changes are necessary for survival, otherwise, one would remain in the periphery. It is because humans are having natural tendencies to explore new and are excited to be the first to use something before others do. The slow changing technology will get less customers as it fails to arouse interest.

2. As explained earlier, the curtain principle leaves a residue for technology too and that residue is the nostalgic people. Thus, the customers are never ending for any slow changing technologies. However, the curtain principle may

not leave any customer for old ones which have never experienced any change. The nostalgia may be only for those who have lived in the time of slow-changing technologies. The short life expectancy of the people (death before 100 years) limits the use of old technology.

3. Though the curtain principle does not leave residue for never changing technologies, it does not allow it to be extinct. It opens the scope of curtaining in some other places such as museum. If the technology sustains itself, the curtain principle will help it to get space in some other field.

4. The curtain principle makes the technology changes unstable. After 1990s, some kind of big invention or discovery is taking place every year which threatens the very existence of the recent technology in the market. This affects both customer who bought old ones and producer who sold old ones. In fact, both expected that this technology would be the

latest but it became an old one within three to five years.

5. The curtain principle can also decide the fate of the technologies born together as twins. The technology which brings more features than the other which released in the same year gets the top position in the market. For example, consider the HD DVD and Blue-Ray Disc which released in 2006. Blue-Ray have won the competition and HD DVD discontinued its production in 2008. The curtain principle also determines which game console becomes victorious in market as the history shows that Xbox, Play Station and Nintendo release in more or less same year or the next year after one.

<u>CURTAIN CONTRACT FOR TECHNOLOGY</u>

To limit the curtaining of technology, all producers can hold a conference or a meeting whereby they promise each other not to make big advances in technology which create instability in the market. However, this contract may result in failure because of three reasons:

1. An individual company can break the contract for establishing monopoly in the market.
2. The scientists and researchers will never stop this work even when the private companies decide to stop. As it is the profession of the scientist and researcher to invent something, he/she will continue to do for livelihood.
3. The customers will demand rapid changes in technology as they will be bored of getting the same technology for use. Thus, the companies may violate the contract to achieve market equilibrium.

This contract can be successful if the following is done.

1. Some monitoring bodies are to be instituted for checking the companies from breaking the contract.

2. The government can introduce alternative employment opportunities for the scientists and researchers to make the existing technology stable in the market.

3. A capitalist state can shift to socialist one for focusing on equal distribution of existing technologies rather than bringing new technologies that divide the society.

QUESTIONS FOR YOUR INTEREST

1. What are the two types of curtain principle for an individual?

2. Why do you think that the micro-units of curtaining are undergoing a declining trend?

3. How is the technology affected by the curtain principle? Discuss the various ways to reduce the impact of curtain principle on technology.

4. Competition and curtain principle are the same and there is no clear-cut difference between them. Do you agree with the statement?

CHAPTER- 2

TYPES OF CURTAINING

DYNAMIC CURTAIN

Sometimes, curtaining overlaps leading to the emergence of multiple things/persons with same features. This means the curtain principle is performed by more than one object/person having same qualities. Some of the examples are given below:

1. The curtaining by 5 big tech giants over the large-scale industries.
2. The curtaining by Unified Payments Interface and Prepaid Payments Instrument over cash.
3. The curtaining by Amazon Alexa/Google Home/Apple Siri over existing voice assistants of just opening the apps in smartphone.

This curtaining is not through a mutual agreement by the curtaining parties. They are different companies and they operate keeping distance from each other. But they all bring the same curtain. This function of dynamic curtain is similar to 'Unity in

Diversity' where all the diverse groups come together against the common enemy.

Dynamic Curtain turns to become a single simple curtain when one of the members of dynamic curtain rushes to overtake the others. But the elimination of dynamic curtain would be a long war between the fighting parties. For example, USA and USSR came together against Nazi Germany in World War II but they fought against each other in Cold War which lasted longer than the dynamic curtaining of Europe by both of them in 1940s. The long-lasting cold war brought USA as the sole superpower in the 1990s which is a result of elimination of dynamic curtain.

SEMI-UNIFORM CURTAIN

The type of curtaining which have same objective but different outcome is called Semi-Uniform curtain. This means that they are having similar aims but they themselves may not be same. For example, the smartphone that many of you use today have curtained the cordless/feature mobile phone of 2000s. Now, there are semi-uniform curtains proposed for curtaining smartphone. They are:

1. Mixed Reality (Virtual Reality + Augmented Reality)
2. Brain chips that can function similar to smartphone

The semi-uniform curtains are also there in international relations such as the attempt by European Union and China to curtain USA but each of them gives different result after the curtaining.

The semi-uniform curtains can be found in history where different kings united against a single emperor but each of them had their own reason.

In politics, opposition party forming coalition governments are forms of semi-uniform curtain.

ACTING CURTAIN

The curtaining also occurs as a simple act to utilize something for a short period after which the original situation is restored. For example, critics say that the US interference in Middle East (West Asia) was for oil resources. For this benefit, they invaded Iraq. But the drama was that the US wanted to disarm Iraq from weapons of mass destruction and to free the people. The US claimed the intention for Iraqi War was to end Saddam Hussein's support for terrorism. Sometimes, US may be true in the claim or may be the critics. Thus, the curtaining by USA made it a famous actor of military power. The word 'actor' is used because it is not permanent but for a temporary nature. There is a true curtain only when something is permanently taken over.

FICTIONAL CURTAIN

The curtaining which is believed to be a fact but actually just the opposite is called fictional curtain. For example, many people think that lower caste have curtained the upper caste which is false. It may be true for small sections of Creamy layer but is entirely incorrect information when applied to larger groups.

The same curtain works with religious groups. For instance, some of the major religions perceive the minorities as majority religious community.

LEGAL CURTAIN

The curtains which are supported by the law of a nation or government is known as legal curtain. This is an unfair and unjust curtain as it is based on discriminatory practices. However, this type of curtaining enjoys immense praise from the foolish experts and scholars who calls it 'positive discrimination' though it is really a 'negative discrimination'. One of the examples that we can cite here is women-oriented policies which leads to aggravation of inequalities and misandry. This curtaining is very dangerous as it can lead to molestation and rape against men by the women.

REVOLUTION CURTAIN

The curtain which is sudden or happens immediately without a notice or warning is called Revolution curtain. People do not even come to know that a curtaining is about to take place. They are hidden and come to the picture only after a curtaining occurred completely. For example, the unexpected cheating by somebody which takes the cheater to heights and deprive the other is a revolution curtain.

RETURN CURTAIN

The curtain which returns the initial top person/organization/phenomena back from bottom to up is called a return curtain. For example, Germany was Weimer republic after the First World War for a brief time. Adolf Hitler turned democratic Germany into a Nazi Germany of dictatorship. Now, Germany again turned into a democracy through a return curtain.

Here is another example. Sometimes, the world's richest person may become second for a short time but is restored to first rank afterwards.

JOB CURTAIN

The curtain which happens in occupations or professions is called job curtain. Some of the jobs that is flourishing now will not survive in future. Much of the physical work can be converted to a digital work. Perhaps, digital work may be turned to something else in the upcoming days. The job curtaining takes place in the following way:

1. **Infant/Baby stage**
    A new job will be first neglected by society when it is launched for first time.

2. **Teen/Youth stage**
    Then, this job gains prominence among those who like to become unique.

3. **Middle/Mature Stage**
    After the unique people become famous, society starts to respect their jobs and then tries to copy.

4. **Old/Eldest Stage**
    The job will become overcrowded and then majority of the people will move to this job. But the selection mechanism limits the number of people entering the job. Unemployment will increase.
    E.g.: Engineering

5. **Dying/End Stage**
    The supply will become equal to the demand. Thus, vacant seats for that particular job will increase, thereby

losing its prestige. People will also start bribing for this job due to which this job will have more professionals having lack of knowledge.

E.g.: Doctor

EXCEPTIONS TO JOB CURTAIN

Some of the jobs which cannot be done digitally or which is dependent by the entire population forever due to their easy access will survive the time. These include agriculture, animal husbandry, poultry cultivation, industries, military and civil services.

You might be wandering why doctor is not an exception to job curtain. It is because when many uneducated or illiterate people use fake certificates for a private clinical practice, the government may come up with a solution where only the best performers or toppers can become a doctor. This will lead to a very less numbers of doctors being selected and the machines will help them to treat a large number of patients. Thus, the doctor: patient ratio is not required to be equal. Robots will assist the doctors in facilitating them. Therefore, some other jobs will curtain the job of a doctor by providing more open seats. However, it is not possible for a robot to replace a doctor because a damage in robot can kill the life of a patient.

There are two types of job curtaining:

1. Inter-job curtaining (Pull factor)

One job curtains the other job. Here, the one job attracts the people working in other jobs or their next generations.

2. Intra-job curtaining (Push factor)

There is a curtaining within the job. Here, the people working in one job is forced to move to another for more income or productivity. The best example for this is teaching field. With the coming of Smart classes (informal term used for video lectures where Information & Communication Technology is applied), the students who have skills in understanding audio-visual content have turned to YouTube and other online platforms for learning rather than learning from teachers/professors. But there are some students who understand live offline lectures than digital materials. They are the ones who forms a barrier to the curtaining of teachers by ICT.

CULTURAL CURTAIN

There is a curtaining of American/European culture on different countries of the world especially India. No countries have found their own way of modernisation except the western nations. You would find many young people criticizing Indian culture and saying that they want India to modernise or else they will leave India and go abroad. The style of dressing by Indian women in the past was Saree/salwar/churidar. However, after globalisation, the women started to wear the clothes not suitable to Indian conditions such as ripped jeans, shorts and shirts. The Indian cinema from 2009 onwards (no clear demarcation as some claim it is 2007) started the new generation which have curtained the old culture. The similar applies to Indian music industry which also became westernised nowadays. The cultural curtain is less in developed countries but it is high in developing countries of Asia and Africa.

QUESTIONS FOR YOUR INTEREST

1. Like a river or a human being, the job also has various stages of life. Comment.
2. Explain the push and pull factors of job curtaining.
3. The Legal Curtaining is unfair though it is legal. Give Reason.
4. Which war is closely associated with dynamic curtain? Explain.
5. Describe the proposals for semi-uniform curtain in technology.
6. A Curtain can be similar to movie acting also. Elaborate.
7. Indian culture is rapidly reducing in its rank on Indian society. Is it right?
8. Rewinding a curtain is possible. Support or oppose the statement.
9. Many curtains among identities are just fictious. Rate and review the statement.

CHAPTER- 3

<u>INFINITE HIERARCHY THEORY</u>

The theory of infinite hierarchy forms the fundamental base of the Curtain Principle. A Hierarchy has no starting or ending. It does not have any boundaries or borders. Intra-Hierarchy movement is flexible and one moves above the order in certain points of time unknowingly. This movement has no regulation and it is called Infinite Hierarchy.

There are the three models of infinite hierarchy:

1. Political Model

There is a hierarchy in every society with the top one being government. Ordinary people's relationship with the government is infinite hierarchy as at a certain point of time, they can change the government and they come to the top of hierarchy. But they have a return march towards down as the hierarchy is flexible. It also means that they can rise again.

This Infinite Hierarchy depends on two factors:

> (a) Courage-Power and Awareness
> (b) Willingness

If people have Courage-Power and Awareness, they will not be ready to accept a hierarchy based on non-merit basis that is unfair and unjust. The government that rules for unlimited period without giving opportunities to the people to change it can be declared unfair. Thus, people can get above the hierarchy to introduce another party at national level and make a country bi-party or multi-party system.

Also, people should be willing to come above the hierarchy without which the infinite hierarchy falls to form a shadow hierarchy.

2. Social Model

When Mahapadma Nanda, a Shudra King came to power during the age of Magadha period, the infinite hierarchy worked in social sphere (in terms of kingship).

3. Cultural Model

For example, films can be taken in the hierarchy model. The Tollywood (Telugu cinema) gone up the hierarchy in 2021 and Bollywood came down the hierarchy. There is also a rise of other South Indian Film Industries.

4. Economic Model

Here, countries can be taken in the hierarchy model. During COVID-19 Pandemic, many countries rise and fall the infinite hierarchy due to fluctuations in economy.

NEED OF INFINITE HIERARCHY

If no more changes are applicable for something or somebody's idea, then infinite hierarchy has to be there for curtaining the useless things or conservatism. Otherwise, people will be fed up of these same ones. Infinite Hierarchy strengthens liberalism and transition.

WHY CHINA HAS A SHADOW HIERARCHY?

Shadow Hierarchy is a concept in which the hierarchy is set within a system which does not include exterior relationships. This hierarchy is rigid and there is no scope for the outsiders (people) to get into it. After the Chinese revolution of 1949, communist party have been ruling the country. Since then, there were protest by many such as Tiananmen square protest in 1989. But all these were suppressed easily. For this, a unity among the people with all the factors of infinite hierarchy is essential.

GUINNESS WORLD RECORDS

The people use their skills to make records in some field by defeating a person of existing top category and earn that status. This is the Guinness World Record which enables the curtain principle to operate but infinite hierarchy too is present. There are people who don't register in Guinness but score more than the Guinness first rank. It may be due to their inaccessibility or lack of interest in getting fame. Sometimes, some people may have a very new skill which nobody else in the world has. This will be underestimated by the society and thus, it does not get recognised because of which one loses confidence in applying for Guinness World Record. It may be also a situation in which there is a lack of money for registering a new skill for the records.

ONLINE CROP CULTIVATION

The online crop cultivation is not related to agriculture. It is cultivation of money through computers or smartphone devices.

There are three types of online crop cultivation:

1. Game cultivation
2. Promotion cultivation
3. Upload cultivation

Game cultivation is of playing games with different persons of the world which need one to deposit some amount of money. If one wins this game, he will get his money back along with profit. But if he fails, he loses all the money that he had deposited.

Promotion cultivation is earning money by promoting other's products. But there is a bad impression created by this cultivation. The viewers of the promoter's website or app becomes angry and hence, they stop using it. So, promoters started a new strategy of subscribing to ad-free package. Here, for a short term, only few people will subscribe and thus, the promotion is successful. In long term, when many people subscribe to this ad-free package, the promotion becomes a failure and the people also develops a hatred towards the advertisements. This requires the promoting platform to give subscription fee to the product owner.

Upload cultivation is the way of earning money when people either download the video/photo or watch (open) it. They depend on visits or subscriptions for money. Here, subscribing for a user is free and the uploader is not working for somebody else.

The role of curtain principle is in changing the rank of these online crop cultivators. Due to rapidity in shifting of ranks, they can lose everything and hence, it will lead to depression, anxiety, change of behaviour, and suicides. The infinite hierarchy is too porous that people have both benefit and drawback in joining online crop cultivation. Therefore, online crop cultivators are dependent on four factors- High speed huge data internet, luck, number & strength of competitors and response by consumers/partners/opposite team.

POST-TRUTH INFLUENCED CURTAIN PRINCIPLE

The Post-Truth determines the popularity of a person/object and its status which indirectly influences the curtain principle. If you see somebody lying about something but he/she don't know that's a lie, then it is post-truth. The rumours and fake news form a part of post-truth. Here, people spread information of the things they are not sure or aware of. This post-truth may be also about the person who is in a higher rank. The negative points about this higher ranked person which is a post-truth will lead to curtaining. The person ranked second can come to first with this post-truth if positive points of this second ranked person are told by the people with each other. Infinite Hierarchy also operate as one moves up or down the order unknowingly due to post-truth.

The Infinite Hierarchy is also taking place when somebody tell a lie. For example, many women make fake cases against men for sexual harassment. This severely destroys the higher ranked status of the person who have been falsely accused by women.

QUESTIONS FOR YOUR INTEREST

1. Express the need of infinite hierarchy in society.
2. Classify the online crop cultivation and explain.
3. Would you consider Guinness world record in curtain principle?
4. Give an account on the models of the infinite hierarchy theory.
5. Differentiate between infinite hierarchy and shadow hierarchy.
6. Justify the relation of post-truth with the curtain principle.

CHAPTER- 4

POLITICS OF CURTAIN PRINCIPLE

The Curtain Principle is not neutral in nature. The behaviour of a competition depends on its difficulty level. There are six types of politics that happen in curtain principle. They are as follows.

1. **To and Fro Politics**

The organisation/person is pushed forward or backward constantly which disturbs the stability of that particular organisation/person. This forces that organisation/person to continue their hard work to secure their position. If he/she/it becomes lazy after getting higher rank, he/she/it will fall down the rank within a short period.

2. **Trap Politics**

The organisation/person who wants to curtain the other makes a trap for the higher ranked organisation/person in the form of a permanent block in its rise. If it is an organisation, then it can be a robbery or a theft. It will affect the fund for that organisation but when the money factor is excluded, the morality of that organisation is not affected. If it is a person, then it can be a murder or assassination of that higher ranked person. There is no decline in rank of the higher ranked person because that person will be remembered by people even after his/her death. But as that person could not do anything more for people, he/she will be ranked the same.

3. Expel Politics

If an object/organisation is permanently discontinued/closed, then it is out of curtain principle. This is usually done when it is lower ranked. The higher ranked will not try to expel itself from curtain principle. If it does so, it is exiting with a profit. This profit would be used to start something new and so, again returns back to curtain principle.

4. Dual Curtain Politics

Sometimes, one low ranked person or organisation tries to curtain more than one high ranked leading to double curtains. This kind of politics is different from dynamic curtains where more than one low ranked person or organisation curtains one high ranked.

5. Multi-curtain Politics

Many low ranked persons/organisations may curtain many high ranked persons/organisations which means that there is a threat from each and everyone in the society.

6. Equal Ranked Politics

Some persons or organisations share the same rank. If they are dependent on each other, then it is complementary. This means that a fall in one's rank will lead to equal fall in the rank of the person or organisation which shared it.

However, there are some persons or organisations that have same rank but are independent of each other. Here, the fall in one's rank will not affect the fall in the rank of the person or organisation which shared it.

MINI CURTAIN POLITICS

The curtaining which is too small to be effective may create a little crash to the higher rank. The higher rank may be classed as 'endangered' or 'vulnerable' to lower rank. So, mini curtain may force the higher rank to adopt some measures to protect itself. It is a message to the higher rank that his/her/its position is in danger. It also generates an experience after which the high ranked person/organisation becomes serious.

Mini Curtain Politics is prominent among political parties. The opposition party may criticize the government by pointing out the illicit activities of the government. This may damage the higher rank of the government. Thus, they have to try their best not to involve in bribing or misappropriation of funds. Therefore, the curtain principle ensures accountability and transparency of the government. The government is responsible to people, otherwise they will be removed by curtain principle.

<u>ADVANTAGES OF CURTAIN PRINCIPLE IN POLITICS</u>

1. The government becomes responsive to people as they are feared of curtaining by other parties.
2. The political parties raise the voice of marginalised, disadvantaged and deprived sections to avoid curtaining.
3. The coalition is usually formed to reduce the impacts of curtain principle. This enables deliberation and debates within a government.
4. The curtain principle gives opportunities for people from lower varna or jati to get into upper rank at least once. The affirmative action is the key to curtain principle.
5. Curtain Principle supports high quality. If anything in politics proves to be clean and standard, that aspect will remain in higher rank until other aspect claims to be cleaner and of higher standard than the former. For example, simple democracy was seen as the best form of government

until recently. But with the emergence of concept of representative & deliberative democracy, ordinary democracy shifted to lower rank.

DISADVANTAGES OF CURTAIN PRINCIPLE IN POLITICS

1. Curtain Principle do not respect the relationships built by the society. There is a competition among all the loved as well as hated ones.
2. Curtain Principle can bring alien invasion as well as colonial rule. The swaraj or independence can be maintained only with improving one's rank from time to time.
3. Curtain Principle makes a twist in the expectations as the party who expects victory may have to face a defeat due to curtaining by other party. The party expects a victory when it has done or promised something good. But some parties make a mistake by ignoring the promise or works/activities of the

others that leads to the operation of curtain principle.

4. The curtain principle is universal which means that it does not have any regional variations. Any competition irrespective of place and time involves the curtain principle without which competition cannot be defined.

CHANGE OF NAMES BY CURTAIN PRINCIPLE

When some rulers politically curtain the other, it changes the name of the kingdom or the country which it is ruling. They do this to show that a new ruler has come to power and attained a higher rank after a long rule by somebody else. Just look how many times Russia has been renamed.

1. Tsardom of Russia (1547-1721)
2. Russian Empire (1721-1917)
3. Russian Republic (1917-1918)
4. Russian Democratic Federative Republic (1918-1918)
5. Russian State (1918-1920)

6. Russian Soviet Federative Socialist Republic (1920-1922)
7. Union of Soviet Socialist Republics [USSR] (1922-1991)
8. Russian Federation (1991- today)

For example, the USSR was named after communist party have curtained all other parties in rank and after they permanently stopped the curtain principle in politics by making a single party system.

QUESTIONS FOR YOUR INTEREST

1. Give example for 'to and fro' politics.
2. Distinguish between multi-curtain and mini-curtain politics.
3. List the advantages and disadvantages of curtain principle in politics.
4. Define trap politics and compare it with expel politics.
5. Contrast the dual curtain politics and equal ranked politics.
6. Mention the various names of Russia that curtain principle have given.

CHAPTER- 5

CURTAINISM

In international relations, there are many theories which explains why the countries indulge in warfare. These are idealism, classical realism, structural realism (Defensive, offensive), Rational choice, and constructivism. But these approaches either overestimate or underestimate the international system like Anarchy and United Nations. Further, these see the nations from the perspective of political or economic dimensions only. Some of these are individualist which see the nations as selfish while others are dependent on the factors of collectiveness of the nations. However, they don't give importance to ranking system which is actually the prime reason for wars.

The curtainism theory states that the countries fight each other for attaining a 'status' (not domination) and to allow oneself or some other lower ranked nations to curtain the higher ranked nation. The curtainism depends on three factors:

1. Competition
2. Revenge seeking
3. Relative Social Progress

Competition

- The various indices like Human Development Index, Multidimensional Poverty Index, Corruption Perceptions Index, Inequality-adjusted HDI and Gender Development Index that is used to compare the nations may lead to an unhealthy competition which causes tensions. These tensions escalate into conflicts that lead to large-scale small wars. Each lower ranked nations try to curtain the higher ranked nation by waging a war. If they fail in the war too, they are able to make some other nation get into a higher rank than their existing targeted higher ranked nation.
- Before these indices were made, the people and rulers of a nation knew which country had higher achievements, thus waging war

against that country to reduce its rank.

Revenge seeking

Sometimes, the countries of higher rank too wage a war against the countries of lower rank. This is to seek the revenge of reducing its rank in the international arena. In this way, the higher ranked country makes gains and the lower ranked country gets loss.

Relative Social Progress

A country may start a war against another country for reducing another country's social progress to that level whereby the country that starts war gets higher social progress than the country that faces war. But there is no absolute social progress of that country. Only in terms of the country that faces war, there is a social progress for the country that starts war and wins in it.

The curtainism is based on curtain principle in the international level. However, it is not on the basis of infinite hierarchy as the wars are a kind of shortcut for attaining higher rank.

CURTAINISM FOR 21st CENTURY

The existing theories of International Relations do not suit the present era. The Curtainism brings a new method of studying IR. It is more relevant because of the following reasons:

1. The Curtainism incorporates social and psychological dimensions also.
2. Curtainism have no motive for establishing a military hegemony nor a peaceful world.
3. Currently, the countries are trying to become a soft power more than a hard power. In this context, the use of hard power is mainly to strengthen the soft power. Thus, curtainism is the only way to help each country attain higher rank so that it become a source of inspiration for those at lower rank.
4. The countries may indulge in war for expansion towards a resource rich area. The Curtainism brings logic in this expansion as the wealth generated from these resources would be used for social progress of

the country that started war which indirectly contribute to the higher rank of that country.

5. The Curtainism is all the causes, process and consequences of the war. It is not an isolated theory of only causes unlike realism.

6. The Curtainism is about 'replacement' and not about 'cooperative', 'collaborative' or 'collective'.

7. The Curtainism do not consider anarchy to be the reason for war. Instead, international statistics, and media reports are regarded to be the chief causes of the war. For example, a small news about weakness of a nation or its resources is enough for a war to start as per curtainism. Nowadays, internet has also increased the wars.

8. The Curtainism seems to be the common cause for all types of conflict like war, genocide, terrorism.

9. The Curtainism include the cyber warfare and digital hacking also. By getting access to another country's

data, one country can get secrets how that country has achieved higher rank, thus leading to curtaining.

10. The Curtainism sees international organisations in two ways: it prevents war but can also become a cause for war. The members of these organisations who are not satisfied can start a war which makes the other members to do a counter-war.

FEATURES OF CURTAINISM

1. The military expenditure increases in GDP with increasing competition in various fields. This was the central reason for Cold War.

2. The Curtainism is overpowered by social media apps such as Facebook, Instagram, WhatsApp etc.

3. The indicators of life expectancy, health, education, happiness and standard of living (purchasing power) are also responsible for war.

4. Comparison, differentiation, and contrasting starkly are all weapons for curtainism.

5. The Alliance formation is not only for security purpose but also for curtaining purpose. The NATO was to curtain the Warsaw Pact during Cold War.

6. The country waging the war is prepared to do any means for any ends. It does not matter whether the action is good or bad and whether the end is failure or success. The aim is to destroy the rank of the targeted country.

7. As curtaining is immoral, the international organisations impose many sanctions on the country practising curtainism. The country doing war loses support from many countries also. This discourages war but still there is an opposing force of encouraging war, that is destruction of other country. The statement goes like this: 'If I fall down, you shall also fall down' or 'If I want a better position, you should have a worser position'.

8. The defence is to prevent curtaining and not attack. Anybody can attack a

country by killing few soldiers but curtaining to get a higher position is not possible if the country is equipped with strong defence. An attack leads to loss of individual lives which is a loss for the family but not for a nation as the military can be supplemented. However, curtaining is a loss for a nation as supplementing force has been destroyed.

9. Horizontal Curtainism works in all vertical order. Curtainism is applicable even for studying the relations between state governments and decentralised bodies like local governments of Panchayati Raj and Municipal Corporations. These are called by various names such as civil war, inter-state border disputes or water/river conflicts. It is because competition is there at all levels. The presence of state cannot ensure the absence of war. However, stateless situation can increase the intensity of a war.

10. Curtainism don't ask a world government because it cannot prevent the war. It can only give instructions or directions for peace. Each nation will raise the issue of autonomy and continue their war. The world that is pushing for decentralisation will not favour a world government.

MULTIPOLAR WORLD BY CURTAINISM

Each country tries to curtain the other for getting higher rank. For this, they assert their power to destroy other's ranks for a prolonged period and that leads to the formation of a multipolar world. Initially, when various indices were not there in the world, the intense competition was only between the higher ranks. That's the reason for the bipolar world until 1990. After few index that compare the countries have been launched, the first decade was of unipolar world as other countries were just trying various methods to improve their rank in the indices. But when all these methods proved to be difficult, they turned to shortcut which was curtainism. There are emerging powers like China which is trying to curtain the West Europe and USA in rank. However, China has not made any improvement in democracy ranking as they prefer to sacrifice this rank to improve rank in other fields.

QUESTIONS FOR YOUR INTEREST

1. Write a short note on the salient features of Curtainism.
2. Prove that curtainism is valid in this 21st century.
3. How do multi polar world result from curtainism?
4. Enumerate the three factors that Curtainism depends.
5. How do Curtainism differ from Realism and Idealism? Also, elucidate the difference between curtainism and constructivism.

> (A Person/organisation who involves in curtaining is called curtainer)

CHAPTER- 6

<u>CURTAINOLOGY</u>

Curtainology is the study of curtain principle. The ideology of curtain principle can be described as follows.

1. The curtain principle is immortal. It even takes place in a communist or Marxist/Leninist/Stalinist economy.

2. The curtain principle does not see rank as 'private'. The ranks are public, as it can be occupied by those having good capabilities.

3. Each property is ranked by people. Higher the rank of a property, the higher is the sale. The rank depends on the utility of the property.

4. The credit for curtaining is not to a single entity. You may have seen higher ranked giving gratitude to someone for the success though that 'someone' don't have much role in the success of high ranked. This is because the society believes that curtain principle cannot be carried out without aid of somebody else.

5. If you respect the high ranked person/organisation, then your rank will improve automatically. The reason is scientific and not grace. For example, the promotion in a job is given only if you respect the high ranked Boss.

GOVERNANCE OF CURTAIN PRINCIPLE

The curtain principle is governed by the following factors:

1. Ability, capacity and talent of low rank to curtain upper ranked person
2. Supplementary entrepreneurship
3. Fault of the higher rank
4. Comment of others about the ranked persons/organisations
5. Command of inner soul

CRITICISMS AGAINST GENDER CURTAINING

Nowadays, the curtain principle operates in gender which is of a big concern.

1. Some feminists demand wages for those women who work in household and do domestic chores. If husband have to pay for work to wife, then wife also should pay to husband for all those things which she uses such as electricity, TV channel price, clothing, water charges and even shelter in the house made by the husband through rent. It kills the natural equality within the family. Thus, curtaining of love for money is dangerous to relationships.

2. The gynocentric society is the prima facie of gender curtaining. Most of the academic textbooks that you use may contain stereotypes. When giving examples, a man would be mentioned as a criminal and a woman as a soft kind hearted person. Also, most of the pronouns used in a book would be 'she' and not 'he/she'. This stereotype is also present in the speeches of academicians.

3. The fact that only one woman has been judicially executed in India after

independence (mercy shown due to pregnancy or being mother) shows how gender inequality persists in India. This proves that women are not equally punished to men in criminal activities. This leads to curtaining by women over men.

4. There are unreported case of women raping men, molesting them and doing sexism against men. Many men are victims of prejudices. But men don't say it openly because they don't want to reduce their rank in society which affects their dignity. The curtain principle obstructs the men from revealing the truth.

5. When men tried to report their sufferings secretly through internet, the governments and companies named them as 'manosphere' and banned them only for improving the rank of feminists in the column of curtain principle. Here, the curtain principle violates the human right to freedom of expression.

- Note: The author supports equal rights for both men and women.

CURTAIN PRINCIPLE IN PAYMENTS

The curtain principle has brought many changes in the popularity of payment methods. The cash was the most popular form of money until 1980s. In 1990s, debit cards and credit cards gained prominence in India though it was introduced much earlier. In 2000s, the POS (Point of Sale) Machine became one of the most advanced technologies for India. In 2010s, the net banking such as IMPS/RTGS/NEFT in the case of India came to be used for distant transactions. In 2020s, QR based scan & pay like UPI (Unified Payments Interface) in India and e-wallets began to be widely used.

RELATIONSHIP BETWEEN QUANTITY AND CURTAIN PRINCIPLE

When the quantity of some goods or species exceeds beyond a limit, the curtain principle reduces its rank. It is because increase in availability (number) is inversely proportional to curtain principle. The goods/species will lose the rank of being 'rare' when the supply increases.

If it is a rare good, producer is not the competitor, instead consumers are competitors. They compete for getting the high ranked good to improve their own rank. For this, they play the game of 'who come first?'. If it is a surplus good, different producers compete for improving the rank of the good that can improve their own rank. For improving the rank of the good, they give discounts. But they ensure that the discount do not go below the minimum rank limit*. If it is a rare species, international community gives higher rank for preventing extinction. But common species is not considered important and hence have a lower rank. It is the humans who bring the lower ranked species to higher rank by hunting them. Thus, curtain principle is also artificially created by the way of poaching.

*Minimum rank limit: If the valuable goods are priced too less, the rank of the goods fall. As everyone can afford to buy, the curtain principle allows the other expensive goods (not too expensive) to curtain the cheap goods. So, the minimum rank limit is the limit on the price decrease of a good to maintain its rank.

<u>CURTAIN PRINCIPLE- DRAWBACKS</u>

A common inference can be that the Curtain Principle is wise as curtaining of one will not ensure safety for the curtainer. The curtainer has to do something to keep with that rank. If not, they will come down the rank and that forces the good to win over evil. However, there are some demerits.

1. There is no permanency nor fusion of a rank with other rank, thus making two ranked distant from each other.
2. Like the sport of football, there is a self-destruction for anything in curtain principle. It means that even if others are not competitive, the curtain principle would continue.
3. The Persons with Disabilities (PwD) or the specially/differently abled people find themselves out of curtain principle. They mostly compete among themselves. Some extraordinary Divyangjan are able to compete with normal people.

4. The curtain principle has set up a comfortable and luxurious life for the high ranked which becomes the sole reason for some to curtain others.

5. After one occupies a rank, then the next upper rank becomes the target and this develops a never-ending cycle of upper rank. The Curtain Principle is the only way to fulfil the greed. Thus, the main cause of greediness is the curtain principle.

6. The Curtain Principle cannot count competitions between entirely different i.e., between gods and creatures, between humans and plants, nor between animals and microorganisms. It is because of the curtain law which states that curtaining is between likes and not between unlike.

7. The Curtain Principle leads to over-exploitation of the environment. It is because many resources will be used by lower rank to curtain the upper rank such as deforestation to make developmental projects so as to curtain other states/countries.

CHAPTER-7

SOLUTIONS TO CURTAIN PRINCIPLE

Since, Curtain Principle is sticked to your lives, you cannot avoid it. However, there are possible solutions so that you can live with curtain principle. They are:

1. Reverse Curtaining Model

If you are curtained by someone, then curtain them back. It is not revenge as your rank has not been decreased. Instead, a new rank is created above you and so, you also have to be curtainer.

2. Changing Status Model

Perhaps, you may not want curtain principle because it creates a negative impression even when you are in a higher rank. Then, change the status of the rank. For example, if the top rank is infamous for corruption, you should not be involved in it.

3. Down To Earth Model

Some people may dislike curtain principle as it makes division in a society based on ranks. You can make friendship with lower rank and converse/talk to them so that you don't feel separated from them. This can be successful if you don't show-off or become arrogant. Giving dignity to other ranks is another way of practicing this model.

4. *Sustainability Model*

The environmentalist can adopt the sustainable curtain principle which is the competition between ranks for highest non-conventional, replenishable and renewable energy. In other words, by changing the nature of competition itself, the curtain principle becomes eco-friendly.

5. *Management Model*

An organisation without a directorate can cause problems which leads to self-depreciation of rank. Thus, the organisations shall appoint highly educated persons into management board so that they take care of the curtain principle and thereby preventing the self-destruction of rank.

6. Naming Model

Some people or organisations try to become better than the first ranked but comes to be known under the name of first rank. This is done by the society to give higher value to the first one who reached that rank. It is because majority of the subsequent ones would be inspired from the first one. The best examples include: 'Kerala Gandhi', '_OLLYWOOD' (fill it with B, K, M, T) etc. This model is good to preserve the rank of the first achiever.

7. Discovery Model (tackle curtainism)

The Curtainism reduces if the countries do not curtain each other for one indicator of development. Each country must invent its own development indicator that rank itself truly as No.1 so that they are self-satisfied.

QUESTIONS FOR YOUR INTEREST

Chapter-6 & Chapter-7

1. Derive the relationship between curtain principle and quantity.
2. Critically analyse the gender curtaining.
3. Detail the drawbacks of Curtain Principle and prescribe solutions.
4. What are the factors that govern the curtain principle?
5. What do you understand by the concept 'Curtainology'? Expand on its ideology.
6. The Payment systems changed with curtain principle. Briefly document the data.

ADDITIONAL INFORMATION

Curtains in Theatres?

There is a ranking system in theatres also. The audience may rank the contestants on the basis of their performance. The curtain is pulled down after the play of each contestant. It is symbolic as the previous contestant sees the next contestant as a challenge to the rank of him/her. If it is a competition judged by experts, then the contestants pray for their own success or some try to do malpractices for victory by disturbing the performance of next. Some remains confident that they will win and nobody will curtain them. The highest rank gets prize or certificate and applause from the audience. In contrast, the lowest rank gets out from the stage forever or the audience may throw some things on them by becoming angry. This theory is used for applying to entire social science field and that is being presented in this book.

It is interesting that as age increases, one goes up the ladder of the different curtain principles and continues until his/her death.

INDEX

*Index is based on the topics of the chapter and not on the repeated words.

www.ingramcontent.com/pod-product-compliance
Lightning Source LLC
Chambersburg PA
CBHW012310240726
48656CB00008B/2629